Custer's Last Stand

Sarah Blackmore

Published in association with The Basic Skills Agency

Hodder & Stoughton

A MEMBER OF THE HODDER HEADLINE GROUP

Acknowledgements

Cover: Dave Smith

Illustrations: Sally Michel

Photos: Mary Evans Picture Library

Every effort has been made to trace copyright holders of material reproduced in this book. Any rights not acknowledged will be acknowledged in subsequent printings if notice is given to the publisher.

Orders; please contact Bookpoint Ltd, 39 Milton Park, Abingdon, Oxon OX14 4TD. Telephone: (44) 01235 400414, Fax: (44) 01235 400454. Lines are open from 9.00–6.00, Monday to Saturday, with a 24 hour message answering service.'Email address: orders@bookpoint.co.uk

British Library Cataloguing in Publication Data
A catalogue record for this title is available from the British Library

ISBN 0 340 77640 4

First published 2000
Impression number   10 9 8 7 6 5 4 3 2 1
Year   2005 2004 2003 2002 2001 2000

Copyright © 1999 NTC/Contemporary Publishing Group, Inc.

Adapted for the Livewire series by Sarah Blackmore

Typeset by GreenGate Publishing Services, Tonbridge, Kent.
Printed in Great Britain for Hodder and Stoughton Educational, a division of Hodder Headline Plc, 338 Euston Road, London NW1 3BH, by Redwood Books, Trowbridge, Wilts

Contents

1 Too Many Indians

It was a hot day.
The month was June.
The year was 1876.

The sun shone on the Little Bighorn River –
a river in North Dakota, in America.

The sun shone on the 225 soldiers
by the river.
They were hot.
They were tired.

The sun shone on their leader.
His name was Custer.
He was hot.
He was tired.

There was a hill in front of Custer.
There were Indians behind him.
The Indians were attacking.
Time was running out.
Custer knew that his men
would have to charge the hill.

The hot sun shone on the hill.
It shone on the Indians on top of the hill.
It shone on their leader, Crazy Horse.

Custer and his men had Indians behind them.
They had Indians in front of them.
They were surrounded.

Clouds of smoke came from the guns.
Clouds of dust came from the ground.
There were only a few soldiers left standing.

Bodies of men covered the ground.
Bodies of horses covered the ground.
Custer was still standing.

General Custer's last stand.

In a short time it would be all over.
Custer and all his men would be dead.

The battle is well known.
It is called the Battle of Little Bighorn.
Custer is also well known.
He is a famous person in American history.

2   The Boy General

Who was Custer?
His first name was George.
When he was a boy
he wanted to be a soldier.

He trained to be a soldier
and joined the army.
Custer fought in the American Civil War.
He showed that he was a brave leader.
He became General Custer
when he was only 25 years old.

Custer was very young to be a general.
He was known as the boy general.
Some people thought that he was very brave.
Other people thought
that he was a bit of a show-off.

He did not always follow orders.
He did not wear army uniform.
Custer wore his own jacket.
It had fringes on.

General Custer wearing his famous buckskin jacket.

After the Civil War,
Custer was given a different job.
He was made second-in-command
of a group of soldiers.
They were known as the Seventh Cavalry.
They worked in the Black Hills.

3   Gold!

Custer found gold in the Black Hills.
He sent one of his men with the message:
'Gold in the Black Hills!'

People rushed to the hills.
They all wanted to find gold.
But there was a problem ...

The Black Hills belonged to the Indians.
It was their land.
It had been given to an Indian tribe
called The Sioux.
Nobody could use the land
without the Indians' permission.

The American government
wanted to buy the land.
They wanted the Sioux to sell it.
The Sioux would not sell.

The Indians were worried
that the land would be taken from them.
They joined with another tribe.
They camped near the Little Bighorn River.
The camp was very big.
There were thousands of men,
women and children.
There were also about 3,000 warriors.

Custer hoped for a battle.
He was keen to fight the Indians.
He wanted to impress
the President of America.

The President was a man called Grant.
Grant had been pleased with Custer
during the Civil War.
After the war they fell out.
Custer wanted to please Grant again.

4   The Battle of Little Bighorn

Custer was given a job.
He was to take his men
and find the Indian camp.
He was told to take his men
to the Little Bighorn River.
He was told to wait there.
He had to wait for other soldiers to join him.

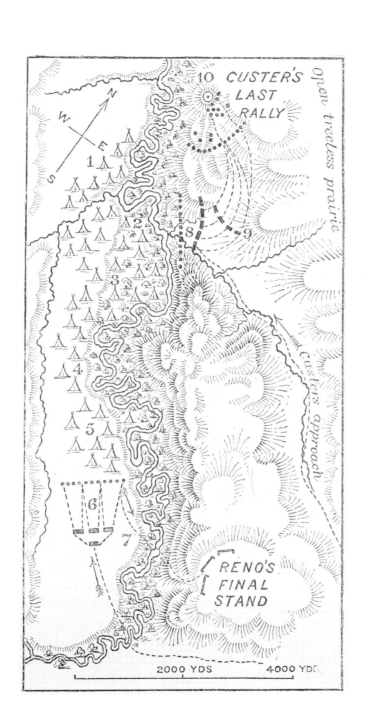

A map showing the Little Bighorn River and Custer's Camp.

Custer made sure that his men
were the first to reach the river.
He found that the Indian camp was really big.
He did not want to wait for the other soldiers.
Even though he did not have enough men
Custer wanted to attack.

Was he brave?
Was he showing off?
Was he seeking glory?

There were too many Indians.
They had better guns.
Still Custer decided to attack.

Custer did not have enough men.
He split them into three groups.

Custer led his group into the valley.
The men were trapped.
Their guns did not work properly.

The Indians kept up the attack.
They did not want to lose their land.
They stopped only when Custer
and all his men were dead.

Even though the Indians won the battle,
there was no real winner.
Soon after the battle
the Indians were made to sell their land.
They were made to live somewhere else.

It was Custer's last battle.
It was Custer's last stand.
It was the Battle of Little Bighorn.